Frederick August Hoffman

A catechism of politics

For the use of the new electorate

Frederick August Hoffman

A catechism of politics
For the use of the new electorate

ISBN/EAN: 9783337134402

Printed in Europe, USA, Canada, Australia, Japan

Cover: Foto ©Suzi / pixelio.de

More available books at **www.hansebooks.com**

A CATECHISM

OF

POLITICS,

FOR THE USE OF THE NEW ELECTORATE,

IN WHICH

Every Question of Political Importance, bearing upon
the Current Events of the Day, is Answered
from a Common-Sense Point of View.

BY

FREDERICK A. HOFFMANN

(*Author of* "*Stray Leaves from Gladstone's Diary,*" "*Shadows
of Coming Events,*" "*Conservative Reaction,*" *&c., &c.*).

LONDON:

WARD & DOWNEY, 12, YORK ST., COVENT GARDEN
1885.

CONTENTS.

TO THE ELECTORS.

It is understood that the General Election will take place in November. The time for preparation has therefore begun. Those will be wise who turn that time to the best account. This can be done by investigating, each one for himself, the questions which are soon likely to be forced on his attention. Let us glance over these questions briefly before examining them catechetically.

First, as to Land. You will be informed by Radical election agents of a proposal by which the farmer and the labourer are to have the first claims on the land, and the owner to have what remains. It is proposed that this theory shall apply to uncultivated land, but, of course, your own sense will tell you at once that the right of *compulsory* cultivation, once admitted, must strike at the ownership of the soil. Plainly the proposal is this, that all land which at any time a landowner cannot let will be taken possession of by the State, and, after the farmer and labourer are satisfied, the balance will be paid to the nominal owner. You will see that this is State-theft and corruption of liberty. You may, perhaps, be a farmer, or a labourer (I presume as well that you are an Englishman), but, to understand the question really, you must place yourself in the imaginary position of a landowner. Then pause to ask yourself why you should be selected as the object of spoliation, while

Mr. Chamberlain, the *patron* of this teaching, should be allowed to enjoy, in purely selfish luxury, the enormous wealth which he has wrung from the sweat of his operatives. Ask yourself why theft should be legalised to deprive you of what you may have bought, or, maybe, inherited from those who bought it for you with their lives and services, while Mr. Bright's fortune, *founded on the long-hour factory system*, the limitation of which, by the Ten Hours' Act, he opposed to the last, and which was *carried in the House of Lords* by the *votes of the Bishops* among other peers, should remain untouched? Remember also, that when farming is bad, either through bad seasons, bad laws, or bad prices, the landlord always feels the first pinch, while the blood-sucking capi-

talists bask with fat-bellied impunity in the
glitter of their own gold. And mark, also,
the danger that lurks in the principle of
the thing. The farmer and labourer are
associated in the question. But ask
yourself: Why favour the farmer? It is
the labourer who works, and, if farmers
lose the support of the landowners, they
will speedily become the prey of the
labourers. And you, who are labourers,
do you imagine then that you will have it
all your own way? Do you think the
Radicals are actuated by a love for you?
No; it is intense hatred of the landowners!
It is hard to tell you that you are being
fooled; but it will be harder when you
come to realise it. The realisation of your
dream will be a life of veritable slavery,
and you will find yourself, like your agri-

cultural neighbours in France, driven by sheer necessity to spend your nights and days in *grinding* and continual work in order to live at all.

SECONDLY. You will hear the House of Lords assailed on the grounds of its past conduct. You will be told that no wonder things are bad, taxes are heavy, landlords are shot in Ireland, and Fenians come over and make disturbances, if there is a House of Lords. You will have leaflets put into your hands abounding in misrepresentations and misstatements, in which the peers will be asserted to have done this, that, and the other, antagonistic to your particular interests. But you will observe that in each case the peers are condemned for " spoiling *Radical* measures," " discrediting

Radical principles," and so on. In every case you will see that the exigencies of party are placed before those of public utility.

THIRDLY, AS REGARDS THE CHURCH. The Radicals are said to be " working to put an end to the special power which the State gives to the Church of England, and they wish to have the enormous wealth of the Church spent for the good of church and chapel alike." Now, before you swallow such nice nonsense as this, you must calculate the gains and the losses which the question will involve. Remember that the secularisation of Church property which Disestablishment means will mean for you the beginning of religion over again from its foundations. Get your friend the parson to tell you the true side of the question before you vote.

FOURTHLY. It is not improbable that Republicanism will be held up as a luscious morsel for innocent ignorance. You must tell your Radicals that if they can get you a Republic without a revolution you will have it, but that you love your lives and your families too much to enter on a bloody campaign which is to give you, in the end, you-know-not-what. Ask them what the new society and the new politics are to do for you—what more they will give you in the way of freedom, morals, literature, or religion. Under the mixed Constitution of this country your lives and property have hitherto been secure; the settled and ascertained opinion of the nation has been sufficient to accomplish all necessary changes. Seek to know, then, for what gain, now, agitation against the Constitution is afloat, private property is attacked, and spoliation advocated. Notice that they promise to *free* anything and everything *that does not belong to them.* Ask them why they do not commence with themselves— start dividing their own enormous riches? If they object to this idea, ask them if they had not better begin by giving the world a new Decalogue?

LASTLY. Attend political meetings and weigh what you hear. You don't want things described by their negatives. See that the idea is made clear, not that it is made affecting to the imagination only.

THE CONSTITUTIONAL PARTY.

"The Tory Party is only in its proper position when it represents popular principles. There it is truly irresistible. Then it can uphold the Throne and the Altar, the Majesty of the Empire, the Liberty of the Nation, and the Rights of the Multitude. There is nothing mean, petty, or exclusive about the real character of Toryism. It necessarily depends upon enlarged sympathies, and noble aspirations, because it is essentially national."—BEACONSFIELD.

Q. What are the primary things which the British Electors will have to consider at the coming election?

A. Whether they will be guided in political life by experience, or by socialistic notions of the Rights of Man and Equality.

Q. What political party do you favour?

A. The party that protects English

interests best, and therefore of necessity
the Constitutional party—nominally "Conservative."

Q. Why of "necessity" in this respect,
the Conservative party?

A. Because the Conservative party is
the only truly National party: in the
words of its late lamented leader—"Un-
less it *is* a National party it is nothing;
it is not a Democratic multitude, it is a
party formed from all the numerous
classes in the realm—classes alike equal
before the law, but whose different conditions and different aims give vigour and
variety to our national life."

Q. Between what political parties will
the electoral struggle lay?

A. Between Conservatives and Radicals
—Constitutionalism and Communism.

Q. What are the respective claims of
each upon the new voters? Have you
nothing to give them but what is already
provided under the Constitution?

A. No; we have no bribes to offer them; we cannot promise to make them perennially happy by the mere magic of an Act of Parliament; we have no plunder to offer them, either from the land, the Church, or the State.

Q. How then do you expect to secure their votes?

A. By simply pointing out to them that *settled order* is their greatest blessing; that if ever they are raised from their present position *they must raise themselves,* for no laws and no parliaments can do it for them; that our land system, our Church system, and other " anomalies," anathematized by Radicals, go down to the very foundations of our Constitution, and cannot be uprooted without such a revolution as would mean for them ruin or even worse.

Q. You will be at a disadvantage. Radical teachings require nothing more than a selfish soul, and a craving

2

stomach to understand them, while the teachings of Conservatism require some knowledge of human nature and history.

A. This is exactly what must be pointed out to them. They must be taught that *they have duties as well as rights;* that as Englishmen they are necessarily citizens of the British Empire, which, founded by Britons, and bought by British blood, should be populated and farmed by British men and women.

Q. Why! there are too many people to live on the land as our fathers did.

A. Just so; but our fathers had not the safe and easy outlet to the Colonies that we have now. How much better would it be for the Radical school to cry " emigration "—for rich and poor alike, who choose —than to preach a system of " confiscation," which must eventually overturn the country, and ruin the people?

Q. It is said, that, bearing upon the

current questions of the day, the Conservative party have no policy?

A. That is a mistake. The Conservative
policy is nothing more than Liberal policy
nationalised. All that is good in the
Liberal programme is to be found in that
of the Conservatives; *it is the method of at-
tainment only which is different*—one revo-
lutionary, the other reformatory.

Q. But during the recent five years'
Liberal reign, what policy had ever the
Tories to offer in exchange for whatever
they may have condemned?

A. It is the business of an Oppposition
to oppose. Yet, apart from the great
questions of Church and State, the rights
of property, the maintenance of the Commons and the Crown—in a word, the pre-
servation, under altered circumstances, of
the mixed constitution of this country, the
Conservative party did intimate the
foreign, the fiscal, and the financial policy
they would pursue when they were in

office. Its fulfilment has, in fact, already commenced.

Q. Can you state the fiscal and financial policy laid down by the Conservatives?

A. These will be found under our heading, " Trade and Taxes."

Q. What are the Conservative views about property ?

A. Briefly, that *no rights are safe where property is not safe.* As in France in the last century, and as in Ireland to-day, punishment, imprisonment and death follow swiftly by some mysterious law on the heels of confiscation. That a policy which sets class against class, and fills all men's minds with disquiet and mistrust, is the most dangerous thing for history, and the poisoner of trade and commerce.*

Q. What are their views on stagnation of trade ?

A. That it means want of capital em-

* " The Tory Policy of the Marquis of Salisbury," by P. H. Bagenall, B.A.

barked in trade; and that attacks on the
security of tenure in property make the
capitalist shrink into his shell. Such attacks have already done a large share of
their evil work. Land is no longer looked
upon as the safest and soundest of all possible investments; capital is being driven
from the land, and we are getting to a state
of affairs in which it will be impossible for
agriculture to survive.

Q. What is their policy respecting Impe-
rialism and Federation?

A. Their policy, as respects the former, is
to open up the markets of the world to this
country, and for this reason they would ex-
tend the empire. Their policy in respect to
the latter will be found under the heading,
" Federation."

Q. What measures have they recom-
mended which may be said to be for the
welfare of the people?

A. Did not the late Lord Cairns, sup-
ported by a Conservative Cabinet, do more

than any other politician to free the hands
of the would be purchasers of land ? Was
not Sir Richard Cross the first to introduce
any really practical plan for dealing with
the re-housing of the poor ? And now, is it
not the Marquis of Salisbury who, by his
speeches and writings, has made himself
responsible for a still larger measure of
reform in this field ?

Q. What do you regard as the most
urgent reform of the day ?

A. The re-housing of the poor. It con-
cerns the social well-being of the people ;
it has deeper philanthropic than political
importance, and we were fully confident that
Lord Salisbury would redeem his pledges in
regard to it. He is doing so.

Q. To what other measures of importance have the Conservatives pledged themselves ?

A. To set on foot an exhaustive enquiry
into the present depression of trade, and to
make a new departure in taxation. Against

the latter the Liberals are arrayed as one
man, and it will be a struggle by the
Conservatives of Right against Might;
but the former is emphatically a question for the working man to decide,
and we feel certain that it will ultimately
become the question which will prove
to the British workmen that the Conservative is the only party which
considers their real as opposed to their
temporary advantage.

Q. How do the Conservatives stand in
relation to the Drink Question? Will they
pledge themselves at the coming election
to assist what is called the " Temperance
Movement."

A. We think so, but at least we hope
they will pledge themselves with discre-
tion. Not long since two members of
Parliament were returned for a large town
solely through the influence of two clergy-
men, who persuaded many of the voters to
reject the proper men because they would

not pledge themselves to assist the "Temperance" cause.

Q. What do you see mischievous in that?

A. Simply this, that those men have since voted for Atheism and the disestablishment of the Church (from which they obtained their support).

Q. Still, as a social evil, do you not think that drink is the greatest?

A. No; English society has many terrible enemies to fear besides drunkenness.

Q. Name a worse evil?

A. Improvident marriages, by which thousands and thousands of poor children are brought into the world to live in squalor and pressing want, and be instructed in the rudiments of crime by their ruthless and reckless parents. Why not then a Church of England Temperance Marriage Society? For the professed support of the so-called "Temperance Movement," we are ready to elect men whose principles are Malthusian,

and whose scripture is the "Fruits of
Philosophy." Abject want is a greater
instigator to crime than drunkenness (nay,
it often leads to drunkenness in the end),
and improvident marriages and profligacy
produce more misery than fermented drinks
Drunkenness is confessedly an evil — a
gigantic evil—but very often it is the effect
as well as the cause of misery. The great
question is to attack the pre-disposing
cause of intemperance. This the Conservative Government has commenced to
do. Meanwhile, in politics, in drink, in
religion, the profession of Conservatives is
Christian liberty.

EQUAL RIGHTS.

"Where there is confiscation or robbery, be it illegal or by legal forms, there confidence will disappear. Where confidence disappears, there industry will perish; and where industry perishes, the labouring man will starve. When these wretched fads have disappeared, there is no one so much as the poorest of the labouring classes who will sympathise with you in upholding that which has made the civilization of England the envy of the world."—LORD SALISBURY, May 20th, 1885.

Q. How do the Conservatives look upon the rights of property ?

A. If honestly acquired, *as sacred and inviolable.*

Q. How do they propose to deal with the holders of such extreme views as " the Rights of Man " and " Perfect Equality " ?

A. By common-sense arguments dealing with the absurdity of their ideas.

Q. Can you tell me who first instituted the theory of " Perfect Equality "?

A. It was the dream of a French philosopher, Rousseau, and has survived only as an effort of the imagination.

Q. Could it be brought within the range of practical politics ?

A. No ; because it is certain that no man is born free, and rarely that two men are ever nearly equal at any period of their respective lives.

Q. Are there any men living who still cling to the practicability of Democratic equality ?

A. Yes, strange to say, men of the literary knowledge of John Morley.

Q. How is this to be accounted for ?

A. Because " equality," as a theory, is favourable to political dogmatism. It is opposed to everything in existence but itself, and, once accepted, saves all need for further enquiry.

Q. You think " enquiry " into the

doctrine of perfect equality would immediately upset it?

A. Assuredly. When a man, by his labour *or services*, has created a value, this value can only pass into the hands of another by one of the following modes— as a gift, by exchange, by loan, or by theft.*

Q. But the Socialists' aim is to enrich *all* classes at the expense of each other?

A. In that case it would come under the latter form, and be simply "theft legalised."

Q. Do not morality and religion make it a duty for men, especially the rich, to deprive themselves voluntarily of that which they possess in favour of their less fortunate brethren?

A. Yes; but that is an entirely *moral* obligation.

Q. Could it not be admitted in practice, or sanctioned by law?

A. No. If it were asserted on principle

* Bastial s " Political Economy."

that every man has a right to the property
of another, the gift would have no merit—
charity and gratitude would cease to be
virtues.

Q. Would equality in respect to the
rights of property be dangerous in any
other way?

A. Yes; it would universally arrest
labour and production; for who would
work if there was no longer to be any con-
nection between labour and the satisfying
of our wants?

Q. Is there any feasible objection to be
raised against the right of inheritance?

A. No. That which a man has produced,
he may consume, exchange, or give, and
what is more natural than that he should
give it to his children? It is this power
which inspires him with courage to labour
and to save.

Q. Why, then, is the right of inheritance
called in question?

A. Because it is imagined that the

property thus transmitted is plundered from the masses. Political economy peremptorily demonstrates that "all value produced is a creation which does no harm to any person whatever; for that reason it may be consumed, and, still more, transmitted, without hurting anyone."

Q. How do you bring equality to bear in respect to the suffrage? Do you see any reason why we should not have manhood suffrage?

A. Yes.

Q. On what grounds?

A. On the grounds of incapacity and irresponsibility.

Q. Why are women prevented from voting?

A. Because they are presumed to be incapable.

Q. And why is incapacity a motive for exclusion?

A. Because the elector does not reap alone the responsibility of his vote; be-

cause every vote affects the community at
large.

Q. Are you in favour of disqualification,
on the same grounds, of paupers, or persons
receiving medical relief?

A. Yes; on the ground taken up by Sir
Charles Dilke, who argues that " to remove
the disqualification would be to take away
the greatest of all inducements which ex-
ists in the country to lead people to join
friendly or provident societies."

Q. Explain this further?

A. If a certain farm-labourer knows that
he shall lose his vote by accepting medical
relief gratuitously, he will be the more
anxious to join a club, which would supply
his need in that respect, or by some other
means prevent himself from becoming
pauperised, and therefore disfranchised, in
case of illness.

Q. The argument, then, in favour of
such disqualification is on the principle of
" self-help "?

A. Yes; of which the Liberals profess to be the staunchest advocates.

Q. Reverting to the question of " Women's Rights "—is it wholly on the ground of incapacity that you object to that doctrine ?

A. Not wholly on that ground, but because the theory is itself contrary to common-sense, and simply flying in the face of Nature.

Q. Explain ?

A. Each sex is personally endowed with physical and mental qualities which fit it for the duties devolved upon it by the ordinances of creation and development, and any straining of these qualities, either in the sense of exaggeration or repression, is opposed to the spirit of the evolutionary law.

Q. Give a more practical argument ?

A. Because it must tend eventually to destroy the harmony of social life.

Q. How do you look upon the question of " Free Land " ?

A. Simply as another form of legalised plunder — a violation of liberty and property.

Q. Do you think the idea impracticable?

A. Yes, not less than pernicious, if we would retain our present state of settled order and government.

Q. What have you to say against a system of peasant-proprietorship?

A. Passing over the theft which such a system would legalise, let me ask, how could it be made practicable? How would the new owners make the system pay without capital, training, or experience?

Q. As to capital, that would be provided by their new masters.

A. Then, surely, the new master of the peasant proprietor—the money lender— would be a worse ogre than the landlord.

Q. But there are cases of peasant proprietorships having paid.

A. That is no proof that the system

3

would pay if applied to the country at
large. Where would be the room for
manufactories, grazing land for large flocks
of sheep, burial-grounds, and so on? If we
could even crystallize such a system into an
experiment, we should only be taking the
first step towards reducing the English
agricultural system to the level of the
Irish. Moreover, ask the tenant-farmer
himself, with capital and experience at his
back, whether he has any ambition to
become a proprietor; he will tell you no,
so long as he can hire land at a return of
ten per cent., for if he set up as a farmer-
proprietor, he would have to sink three-
fourths of his money in the land at two
per cent. and would only receive ten per
cent. on the remaining quarter. Yet what
is impossible for the practical farmer, the
Radicals expect to make a possibility for
the labourer.

Q. Why then should these men wish to
force such a scheme upon us?

A. It is simply an attack upon the land-owners; to depreciate the value of landed property, and serve as an electoral bait.

Q. But, Sir Charles Dilke, referring to the condition of agricultural labourers, declares that " the holding of large estates decreases in various ways the agricultural yield of the country." If this is the case, the large landowner is the right person to be attacked.

A. Let this be admitted. But evidence attests just the other way. The system of large farms allows the profitable use of labour-saving machinery, ensures the clearing away of useless hedges and ditches, and the utilisation of every square yard of land; it results in good roads being made, in the best manures being used, and generally in the extraction of the largest possible amount of produce from the soil. If indeed this draining, enclosing and cultivating of marsh and fen be theft, let the Radicals explain what

3*

theft is. Small holdings, cultivated by peasant proprietors, would mean spade labour, the most profitless form of husbandry; it would mean the practical extinction of the larger agriculture, such as grain-growing and stock-raising, in favour of the smaller ; such as the cultivation of cabbages and potatoes. It would reduce our annual supply of home-grown food by more than one-half, and throw us more and more upon the mercy of the foreigner. As a system, it is directly opposed to every principle of political economy.

Q. But Sir Charles Dilke declares it to be a question above all economics.

A. Then he is not a disciple of Mr. Cobden. Either we decide these questions of political economy or we do not. If we do, then peasant farming stands condemned on the best evidence. If we do not, then the system of large estates may claim to be pressed on grounds such as those on which not only Lord Beaconsfield, but Mr. Gladstone, has defended them. If we look to moral results in the one case, we may look to moral results in the other ; and " the good moral effect of a resident gentry, possessed of what, in the Radical philosophy, are large estates, is attested by evidence which only a bigot could resist."

Q. You think, then, equality in wealth and comfort simply a pretty ideal ?

A. That is all. If we can get plenty of work, and a good price for doing it, we ought to think ourselves well off, and this is exactly what the Conservative Government are trying, against many difficulties, to get for us. Mr. Chamberlain, embar-rassed by his own ideals, has just said " he does not believe that there can be absolute equalities of condition," yet he is the very man whose teaching has impeded the pro-gress of industry and labour.

TRADE AND TAXES.

"The time will come when the working classes of England will come to you on bended knees and pray you to undo your present legislation." — DISRAELI, speaking on Free Trade, 1852.

Q. What are Cobden's arguments and the arguments of his followers founded upon?

A. The arguments of the Cobden Club are founded on the false foundation that, if we can buy the smallest fraction cheaper abroad, the employment of the working classes is of no consequence.

Q. Is that not a sound policy?

A. No. The loss is far greater to the State than the gain, because the State loses the wage-earning and tax-paying powers of the thousands of unemployed operatives.

Q. Do you consider Free Trade injurious to the interests of the working man ?

A. If you mean the one-sided Free Trade that England is at present enjoying (?), we say " Yes."

Q. Why?

A. First, because it is useless for the artisan to bring up his children to any industry that can be carried on abroad.

Q. They can carry their brains and labour to other countries?

A. This has been tried, and what is the result? We are beaten in our own markets. Our shops are full of foreign goods.

Q. Yet, during the last twenty years our trade has increased many millions.

A. Truly, and the Board of Trade returns show that other countries have quadrupled their exports at the same time.

Q. But, then, we have by far the largest trade, have we not ?

A. Yes, and by far the greatest need of it. Moreover, our nation *depends* upon its foreign trade—France, Germany and Russia can live without it.

Q. You mean they are self-supporting?

A. Yes, so far as the essentials of existence are concerned.

Q. But without trade they would be poorer?

A. Truly, but they would lack neither food nor clothing. Under *our* Free Trade we have converted ourselves into a vast hive of artisans, prosperous so long as our work sells, but without resource when it fails to find a market.

Q. But the system of Free Trade, according to Political Economy, is simply an extension of the principle of the division of labour.

A. That means *universal* Free Trade, but not an isolated and one sided policy such as ours. *If* countries trade freely with each other, the natural consequence is that each nation gradually increases the production of those commodities for which circumstances have specially adapted it, and at the same time decreases the manufacture of those commodities for which it has no particular facilities for producing, thus diminishing the cost of production.

Q. But England, having taken the lead, is it not likely that other nations will, in time, follow her example?

A. It is not unlikely, but that will not be in our day, nor in that of our children ; and it is with these that we are immediately concerned.

Q. Still, you admit the possibility of such a condition of trading eventually?

A. The *possibility.* But, meanwhile, our trade is becoming year by year less expansive in proportion to the increase of our population. The future of English trade is darker still, for it is becoming every year more dependent on the export of coal and iron, not to be replaced, and of its

capital to be employed in other countries
in working up the exported raw material
of the land. How long can this last? It
is the duty of English statesmen to legis-
late for England and her dominions; to
be *national* first, and cosmopolitan after-
wards.

Q. How do your arguments bear upon
agriculture?

A. We answer by asking how long this
country can continue free imports in corn
with heavy duties payable to foreign States
on her manufactures? Can any system of
tenure meet the loss on depreciated produce, caused by low prices and unrestricted
competition?

Q. How would the Conservatives deal
with the depressed state of agriculture and
manufacture?

A. They would propose a modification
of the system of free imports, and the
adoption of regulated tariff duties on imports; but Lord Salisbury considers a corn

law of any kind impracticable as well as undesirable.

Q. Why?

A. Because the quantity of corn produced in this country is so much below what is required for the daily food of the population, that to import foreign corn is a necessity; that if a corn law were enacted, it would be of so precarious a character that the disturbance of, and uncertainty to, agriculture would be more damaging than any probable advantages likely to follow. Even the competition for labour in towns is aggravated by the influx of agricultural labourers, and generally of persons born in rural districts, into the towns.

Q. What is the reason of the latter?

A. That corn land being turned into grass land, instead of three men to a hundred acres, one man is sufficient.

Q. But it is proposed that, so as to enable landowners and farmers to compete against foreign agriculture, rates and taxes should be reduced, that the general taxation of the country should be raised from the general wealth of the country, and not mainly from what is called real estate and capital invested in agriculture.

A. Yes, that was attempted in Mr. Childer's defeated Budget. But have you read what Lord Salisbury says of such a proposal? "It is quite right," he says, "that lands and houses should pay their fair share, but I should like it to be remembered that lands and houses already pay an enormous surplusage of taxation in the form of rates. The legislation which puts all the burden of rates on that one solitary interest is one of the great blots on our financial legislation.*

Q. How was it that Free Trade was prosperous for so many years under

---

* This is instanced by Lord Salisbury in his speeches at Welshpool and Hackney in April and May 1885.

Peel's policy of Free Imports and direct taxes ?

A. Times were different ; the productive forces of the world have marvellously changed since 1842, but high tariff duties against this country are continued, and in most cases increased. Who can say now that there is a single national and industrial trade thriving ? Peel's policy is exhausted, and only those whose reputation depended on its success remain to defend it.

Q. You think, then, one country should deal with another on equal terms ?

A. Yes. If we import foreign goods, we should compel foreign nations to take our own manufactures free also. By the duties we are called upon to pay we simply support the armaments of other countries, which we can little afford. In 1842, Peel himself said that the free import theory would be made more advantageous to this country by a corresponding policy in duties imposed on British manufactures by other countries, and that this country had a right to ask for that advantage. These are the very lines upon which the Conservative party advocate free trade, contending, like Peel, that no abstract theory ought to bind a nation's import duties.

Q. But yet hundreds of free-traders at the present day think it heresy to raise taxes by import duties.

A. Yes, and if war happened to occur, say between England and Russia, how long would your present system of free imports be continued? The past would be repeated, and there would be import duties and subsidies to allies. The free trade theory was always associated with peace. Cobden looked complacently to the future as a period of peace and extended trade. It was the dream of a visionary.

Q. But war has been avoided?

A. For the present; who will foretell

the future? And certainly, if once entered on, it would shake the theories and falsify the prognostications of the free trade school of economists to the uttermost. There are interests beyond the mere sale of cotton goods, and even cheap or low-priced foreign corn. Bread is a great blessing, but it is of little worth if the poor man has no money to buy it with.

Q. You think it impossible, at least, then, to guarantee a permanency to our commercial system?

A. Yes; our export trade can only last while other nations continue to purchase of us, and becomes less and less every year. When this fails, with its accompanying diminution of labour, where will the maintenance fall?

Q. On the land.

A. And if the land cannot defray the expense of its cultivation?

Q. You think, then, that the respective merits of "Free Trade" and "Protection" have undergone a change since the last generation?

A. Without a doubt. While the disciples of Adam Smith, Mill, and others, were all impassioned Free Traders, the masters of modern economic science are inclined to speak of Free Trade with dubious approval; and more than one of them hints that even the theory—contradicted as it is by facts—needs revision. Free Trade in words, involving benefits to Radical sections of the community, is more consistent with feudal times than with this Victorian age. If we are to continue in competition with the Continent, let us carry no more taxation than our continental neighbours, and then we can go on successfully. Whatever may be said of Free Trade, Cobden's " Free Trade " is a failure, on the authority of experience, local losses, and bullion statistics.

EXPENDITURE.

"I charge them with the mismanagement of finance and an extravagant scale of expenditure."— W. E. GLADSTONE, December 1st, 1879.

"You were offered in 1874 the repeal of the Income Tax. . . . We were ready to repeal the Income Tax."—W. E. GLADSTONE, November 29, 1879.

Q. In whatever other particulars the Liberal Government may be allowed to have been weak, you will of course admit that they were strong in finance?

A. Certainly not; since they were unable to maintain the principles to which they were pledged.

Q. In what respects?

A. Five years ago, Mr. Gladstone, de-

4

nouncing the faults of his predecessors, asserted one principle with the most unbending sternness; it was that, "If you wish to have a sound and honest finance you must pay your way"— that is, you must take care the balance is on the right side at the end of the year. Now, the balance left uncovered by the last Liberal Budget was £7,432,000, while, in the Chancellor of the Exchequer's own words, his deficit was the largest which had been placed before the House of Commons since the Crimean War.

Q. Compare the expenditures of the Government of Lord Beaconsfield and Mr. Gladstone.

A. Mr. Chamberlain's own figures show for the Liberal Government an additional expenditure of 54½ millions, or an average of nine millions more per annum than the expenditure of the Conservatives.

Q. But you must allow for difference of circumstances?

A. This we do: we say nothing to the soundness of the principle laid down by Mr. Gladstone in 1879. No man can deny that it is a prudent thing to restrict expenditure within the limits of income, though there are times when even a prudent man may borrow to meet a pressing necessity. But the stern moralist who lays down an inflexible rule of conduct, and applies it rigorously to others, ought not to be the one to abandon his own principles the moment the strain comes which ought to prove their strength.

Q. You contend that if any elasticity were to be permitted in its application, that circumstance should have been properly recognised in the criticisms applied to the Conservative Government?

A. Yes; it is Mr. Gladstone's dereliction of principle that raises contempt. Take again the subject of taxation. On the 29th November, 1879, Mr. Gladstone said: "We are not fond of taxation;" yet, in the whole of the last administration, according to their own figures, the Liberal Government took from the British taxpayers forty-one millions more in taxes than the Beaconsfield Government did in the same space of time, or an average of nearly £7,000,000 more per annum.

Q. But the Government had to pay off the whole of the war charges, bequeathed to them by the Conservatives, and which amounted to half a-million a year.

A. Well, let that be deducted from the nine millions extra expenditure, there was still an increase of six and a half millions per annum against the Gladstone Government, while, after *all* " Tory legacies" have been paid off, the estimated Liberal expenditure was nearly a hundred millions sterling.

Q. But, under the circumstances, that was a necessary demand.

A. Yes; and thus we have brought home to our minds the real bearing of the

Egyptian and Russian questions. There is indelibly written on our memories the £25,000,000 *wasted* on Egypt and the Soudan, the £20,000,000 spent in rolling back the war-cloud from our Indian Empire, which ought never to have been allowed to gather; the £100,000,000 budget, which ended in the late Government defeat, and the £15,000,000 deficit. It disposes, once and for ever, of the Liberal boast of superiority in matters of finance. Every one of the "canons of finance" enumerated by Mr. Gladstone at Midlothian, were, like the rest of his promises, broken. Even the method of meeting their increased expenditure shows an entire want of financial ability. It was to be met simply by adopting the rough and ready process of taxing the taxed. Increased burdens were to be given to the already over-burdened, and neither ingenuity nor charity was exercised in effort to distribute the weight, though many plans were suggested for making those who indulge in luxuries pay for the luxuries they can afford. It is to be hoped the electors will bear these things in mind.

Q. Apropos of this, what have you to say to Mr. Chamberlain's suggestion of raising revenue by a graduated income tax or house tax?

A. We should say in Mr. Gladstone's words that " it would be an unjust and wicked impost."

FEDERATION.

"Is it not a sorry sight, with the fact that our Empire boasts of 250 million subjects facing us, that a desultory warfare in the deserts of Egypt, with semi-barbarous Arabs, necessitated recourse to the Guards, and that the despatch of less than 10,000 men should so strain our resources as to require a Royal proclamation to call out the Reserves, the Militia, and possibly the Volunteers."—*Vide* Press, May, 1885.

Q. Do you think the agitation for "Federation" a favourable sign?

A. A most welcome sign; it would largely remedy the evils of which we have but now been speaking.

Q. What would you mean by the term "Federation"?

A. Do you mean Federation as affects

those constitutional questions which belong to its various provinces?

Q. No; exclusively as it is applied to the British Empire.

A. In that sense we take it to mean the settlement of obligations and rights for the welfare of the whole body politic, the blending into one harmonious whole of our Imperial interests—in plainer language, the check and prevention of disintegration, and the utilization for its benefit of all the products and forces of the Empire.

Q. Why do you think the idea of Federation is one born in good time?

A. For some time England pursued a policy of disintegration. The disestablishment of the Irish Church was pregnant with serious consequences. It was a first indication that the bonds of union were to be relaxed. It was a fatal admission that Ireland was a separate country, its people a separate people, requiring special treatment, different laws, different ecclesiastical arrangements. It dealt with Imperial questions in a way dangerous to stability; it was a premium on agitation of a most mischievous kind; it implied that Ireland was a nation instead of part of a nation, and that she had distinctive natural rights, which it was then prophesied truly would culminate in a demand for autonomy.

Q. Do you think Mr. Gladstone foresaw the results that would arise from his action towards the Irish Church?

A. No; it is to be questioned whether Mr. Gladstone felt even the responsibility of his act. Look at his manifest indifference towards our Colonies and dependencies; cast your thoughts on India, South Africa, Egypt, Australia. We seemed, during his late ministry, to have taken very subordinate views of the political matters that engaged not only our attention but the attention of other countries.

Q. You mention Egypt. In what respect are our colonial relations affected by Egypt?

A. In respect to the Suez Canal and our trade route to India and Australia. Our insular position, our supremacy at sea, and the discovery round the Cape of Good Hope, have given us an independent position, with ready access to all the countries of the world, and enabled the products of our industry to compete on favourable conditions in all markets, even under the unfavourable influence of hostile tariffs. Thus, we rightly feel the importance affecting our control of the Suez Canal, and our relations with Egypt are at present very questionable.

Q What would a Conservative administration have done with regard to Colonial policy under similar circumstances?

A. It would have recognised and maintained the Queen's supremacy in South Africa; strengthened our defences of India by retaining Candahar; and used the

inheritance, bequeathed by Lord Beaconsfield, of honourable peace and perfect amity
with the civilised world by acts of commercial enterprise and civil importance,
It would probably have devoted its
attention to the question of the gradual
development of the railroad system, which
at no distant date will connect Europe with
Asia.

Q. With what object ?

A. As Russia advances to the frontier of
India, and extends her railroad system in
that direction, one of the results will
probably be to bring India into more or
less direct communication with the railway
system of Europe, and to give the manufactures of Germany a ready access to the
markets of the East.

Q. But there are some—many amongst
the Radical school of politicians—who
think the Colonies a burden upon the
mother country ?

A. Yes ; but facts, you see, point to the

contrary. It is amongst the first and most vital problems of the day, how the Colonies and the mother country can mutually aid each other, so that, in an Imperial sense, there may be a vast industrial country, producing and distributing wealth for the gain of the whole. India and the Colonies have the means of amply supplying the home market with agricultural produce.

Q. Would not this be impossible under absolute free trade ?

A. Certainly it would. The Colonists are not free traders, and to *wait* until they become so would be to practically abandon Federation.

Q. In this instance you think, then, it is the old State that has most to gain ?

A. Assuredly ; for it can, without loss of dignity, and evident advantage, meet the industrial wants and wishes of the Colonies. There can be no doubt that recent events as well as the emphatic testimony of men like Lord Rosebery, Mr. Forster, and Mr.

Goschen have done much to bring home to
English people what the colonists, for their
part, are not likely to forget—that the
welfare of the mother country and of the
Colonies depends on their close union. This
is the lesson which, above all, requires to be
taught to the workmen of the towns and
the new electors of the counties. To show
those who are naturally inclined to vote for
limiting and cutting down the responsibili-
ties of the country, that if the empire is
allowed to shrink, trade will shrink with it.
It is not "lust of empire" that is sought, but
the interest of the trading classes. We have
got Canada, and South Africa, and Australia, and India, and if we would continue
our world-wide commerce, we must keep
them.

AN APOLOGY FOR THE LIFE

OF THE

RIGHT HON. W. E. GLADSTONE;

OR,

THE NEW POLITICS.

" You go not till I set you up a glass
Where you may see the inmost part of you."

OPINIONS OF THE PRESS.

" *The book is both instructive and interesting, and it is especially valuable in view of the coming general election. It ought to be placed in every Conservative and Liberal club in the kingdom.*"—Bury Guardian.

" One of the most comprehensive and powerful indictments against Mr. Gladstone that has ever been issued."—*England.*

" A clever book. . . . Though severe in his judgments he is scrupulously accurate in his statements of fact, and very rarely passes what may be termed the line of fair criticism."
—*Nottingham Guardian.*

" This is a cruel piece of work. The writer's accuracy is quite unimpeachable, and he has collected his facts with such industry, and marshalled them with such skill, that the book would have been crushing if Mr. Gladstone had any reputation to lose."—*Vanity Fair.*

"A clever, if merciless, account of the life of the ex-Premier, judged from a Conservative point of view, with a rather scathing commentary on his sayings and doings from the year of his birth, compiled by the journalist who wrote 'Letters to My Son Herbert.' To Conservatives this volume will be a perfect mine of information."—*Publishers' Circular.*

"Partly biographical and partly satirical, this is a very clever production."—*Edinburgh Courant.*

"The author of the book pursues Mr. Gladstone pitilessly throughout his political career, every event of which he causes either to adorn a tale or to point a moral. The book distorts nothing and conceals nothing. . . . Appropriately published at the present time, as it demonstrates at once lightly and laboriously the long course of political imposture by which Mr. Gladstone has become famous."
—*Bristol Times and Mirror.*

"A bitter attack on Mr. Gladstone and all his doings from the day of his birth . . . No doubt this book will be used as an armoury from which weapons may be drawn by Mr. Gladstone's opponents."—*Hampshire Telegraph.*

"The book will hardly amuse Mr. Gladstone, if he can be induced to read it, but it will irritate many of his admirers."
—*London Figaro.*

WARD & DOWNEY, Publishers, 12, York Street, Covent Garden, London.

www.ingramcontent.com/pod-product-compliance
Lightning Source LLC
Chambersburg PA
CBHW021631270326
41931CB00008B/964